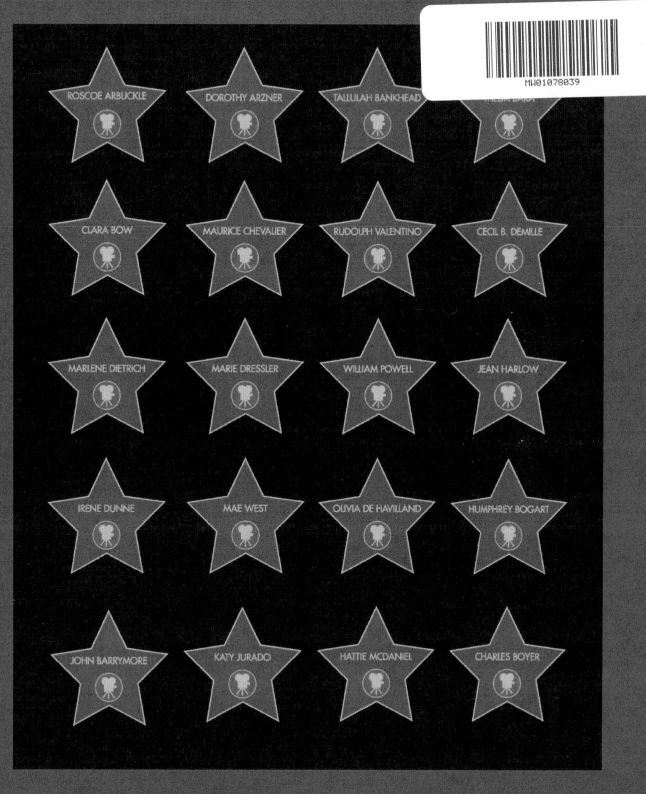

DEDICATION

"Movies Are Magic" is dedicated to all of you fabulous cinephiles, noiristas, film historians, and classic movie fans out there. Thank you for keeping these incredible works of art alive.

MOVIES ARE MAGIC

Written by **Jennifer Churchill**
Illustrated by **Howell Edwards**

Introduction by
**Turner Classic Movies
Primetime Host Ben Mankiewicz**

FROM THE AUTHOR

This book provides an introductory glimpse into the fascinating history of where the streaming images kids watch on digital devices today can trace their origins.

It is my hope this book will make families want to watch these classic films together. And I hope it inspires kids to appreciate the beauty of the communal aspect of watching movies in a dedicated space, up on the big screen, together with strangers and friends.

As Norma Desmond infamously says in "Sunset Boulevard" about the magic of being a movie star ~ It's "just us, the cameras, and those wonderful people out there in the dark!"

INTRODUCTION

Ben Mankiewicz, Turner Classic Movies Primetime Host

For better than 15 years, I've been a host of Turner Classic Movies, so for a decade and a half, I've experienced the power of this singular connection between the channel and movie lovers. I love sports, but I feel no kindred spirit with ESPN; I love *Breaking Bad* and *Better Call Saul*, but do I feel an emotional connection to AMC? Of course not.

There is something special about TCM, about how these classic movies link us to our younger selves, to our parents, to our grandparents, to our collective history. All of us who love *Casablanca* and *Citizen Kane*; *Butch Cassidy and the Sundance Kid* and *Baby Face*; *Random Harvest* and *Requiem for a Heavyweight*; *Sabrina* and *The Searchers* dream that we'll successfully communicate that passion along to the people we love most, especially our children. And that's what this book does – it passes the love forward, giving children a chance to safely experience the exhilaration and magic of Bogie and Bergman, of Newman and Redford, of Greer Garson and Audrey Hepburn.

Few daydreams bring me more joy than imagining my daughter looking up at me and asking, "Daddy, can we watch *Singin' in the Rain* again?"

When it happens, I suspect I'll have this book to thank ... along with forcing her – for years – to watch her father introduce these movies on TCM.

THEDA BARA

CECIL B. DEMILLE

JEAN HARLOW

HUMPHREY BOGART

CHARLES BOYER

MOVIES ARE MAGIC

Do you watch cartoons, TV shows, or movies?
Do you go to movie theatres?
Do you watch videos on your mom's or dad's smartphone?
(Not too much, though, right?!)
Maybe you watch videos or movies:

HOLLYWOOD BLVD.
1910

- ⭐ In your living room
- ⭐ In your bedroom
- ⭐ In the bathroom (!)
- ⭐ At the park
- ⭐ In the car ... or
- ⭐ At the beach.

Movies are magic because they are fun and part of our daily lives.

SUNSET BLVD.
021

Watch This Movie / Miren Esta

"The Gold Rush"
starring Charlie Chaplin, 1925

DOROTHY ARZNER

MAURICE CHEVALIER

MARIE DRESSLER

MAE WEST

KATY JURADO

SHARING STORIES

Since the beginning of time, people have needed to tell each other stories. People tell a story when they:

- ⭐ Talk, sing or act
- ⭐ Draw pictures
- ⭐ Make art
- ⭐ Write letters and words

Movies and videos are the most popular way people tell stories today. When movies first began, there were no computers, no videos, and no TVs.

The only way to see a movie was to go to a theatre and watch it with other people.

Did you know movies are an optical illusion? This 1800s toy, a zoetrope, has pictures inside that look like they are moving when you spin the top. This trick of the eye is called "persistence of vision." It's why we think movies are moving, and one more reason they are magic!

Movies are magic because they bring people together.

VAUDEVILLE FUN

Before movies were invented, vaudeville shows entertained people and made them laugh.

People went to local theatres to see dancers, magicians, singers, clowns, and dogs dressed in silly costumes.

Many of these performers later became the first movie stars.

Movies are magic because of talented vaudeville performers, the heart of show business.

A HORSE, OF COURSE!

Horses helped invent movies. One day in 1879, a very rich man in California named Leland Stanford hired an inventor to find out the answer to a mystery. He wanted to know if all four hooves of a horse ever left the ground at the same time.

The inventor's name was Eadweard Muybridge (yes, he spelled his first name like that!). He set up a bunch of cameras on a racetrack. Each camera took a single picture as a horse ran by. And guess what? One photo showed all four hooves off the ground at the same time! The human eye could not see this.

If you print and cut out these horse pictures, and then flip through them really fast, it looks like they are running.

This is called the Phi Phenomenon. And it helped give people the idea to invent movies.

Movies are magic because they make pictures move.

LE VOYAGE DANS LA LUNE

In 1902, French film director Georges Méliès [*pronounced Zhujsh Mel-ee-ays*] took "A Trip to the Moon." This fantasy story is so creative!

There is a modern children's movie called "Hugo" directed by Martin Scorsese. It is all about Monsieur Méliès! He was an amazing artist and an inventor.

Before "A Trip to the Moon," the Lumiere Brothers showed a movie in 1895 that was less than one minute long. It showed people walking out of a factory after work. At first, most movies only showed simple things like bears dancing or trains arriving at a train station.

That's why Monsieur Méliès' movies were so amazing. He was the first film director to make movies tell a story.

Watch This Movie / Miren Esta Película

"A Trip to the Moon"
directed by Georges Méliès, 1902

Les films sont magiques car ils font des rêves une réalité.

SOUND OF SILENCE / SILENTS

At first, these "moving pictures" had no sound.

We now call these first films "silent movies." But they weren't really silent. Musicians would be at the theatres to play music to go along with the action of the movie. The music could make the sound of a door slam, or glass breaking, or make the movie sound happy or sad.

A silent movie about airplanes won the first Best Picture prize at the first Academy Awards in 1929. The awards ceremony happened in the Blossom Room of the Hollywood Roosevelt Hotel. The name of that first Best Picture movie is "Wings."

Movies are magic because you can watch them with a live orchestra.

Watch This Movie/Miren Esta Película

"Safety Last"
starring Harold Lloyd, 1923

Watch This Movie / Miren Esta Película

"The General"
starring Buster Keaton, 1926

SILENT STARS

Silent movie stars were very talented. They couldn't use their voices. So they used their faces and actions to tell stories. These silent actors and actresses were the first movie stars.

Some of the most famous were Mary Pickford, Douglas Fairbanks, Harold Lloyd, Buster Keaton, Charlie Chaplin, Clara Bow, Lillian Gish, Gloria Swanson, Marion Davies, Greta Garbo, Colleen Moore, Marie Dressler, Mabel Normand, Norma Shearer, Pola Negri, Dolores del Rio, Rudolph Valentino, John Gilbert and John Barrymore.

Movies are magic because they don't need sound to make you laugh.

SOUND OFF!

Finally, "talkies" were invented! The first feature film with sound was made in 1927. "The Jazz Singer" was a musical starring singer Al Jolson. It amazed audiences using a new sound system called Vitaphone. It was the end of the silent movie era.

The next year, Mr. Walt Disney introduced a certain mouse character to the world in the first full sound cartoon! If you ever visit Disneyland, you can watch "Steamboat Willie" in a little movie theatre near the park entrance.

Movies are magic because they can be shown with sound and music!

WOOF!

THE
JAZZ
SINGER
I WAS BLUE, JUST AS BLUE
AS I COULD BE, EV'RY DAY
WAS A CLOUDY DAY FOR ME

SPANISH DRACULA

Classic movies were filmed in France, Brazil, Mexico, Germany, Russia, India and many other countries. They were also made in many languages.

In 1931, there were TWO versions of "Dracula" filmed in the United States: One in English and one in Spanish. The Spanish version was made on the same movie sets, but at night with different actors! Both versions are very good movies, but maybe just a little bit scary.

Las películas son mágicas porque están hechas en muchos países alrededor del mundo, y se pueden apreciar en muchos idiomas.

DANCING WITH STARS

Fred Astaire and Ginger Rogers were famous dancers and singers in movies called "musicals." Fred and Ginger would practice for weeks and weeks for their dance scenes.

Fred was more famous, but many people point out that Ginger "did everything he did, but backwards and in high heels."

In the famous movie "Top Hat" from 1935, their fancy moves will make you want to jump up and start dancing yourself!

Movies are magic because you can dance to them.

Watch This Movie / Miren Esta Película

"Top Hat"
starring Fred Astaire &
Ginger Rogers, 1935

THE NICHOLAS BROTHERS

Two dancers who were even more talented than Fred & Ginger were the Nicholas Brothers. Fayard and Harold grew up watching their parents perform in vaudeville shows.

The two brothers could jump high into the air and land in the splits! Their style of dancing was called "flash dancing."

Movies are magic because we can see the amazing talent of people from many, many years ago.

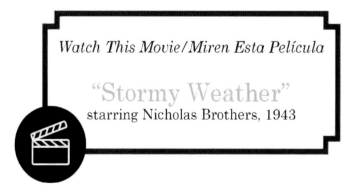

Watch This Movie / Miren Esta Película

"Stormy Weather"
starring Nicholas Brothers, 1943

MOVIES IN COLOR

Movies were only made in black and white for many years. But in 1939, two blockbuster movies were shown in bright, vivid color.

"Gone With the Wind" was about the Civil War. It was the movie version of Margaret Mitchell's very famous book. The big movie stars in this movie were Vivien Leigh and Clark Gable. Hattie McDaniel also starred in this movie. She was the first African American to win an Academy Award.

Another very famous in-color movie people first saw in 1939 was "The Wizard of Oz." It was the movie version of L. Frank Baum's popular fantasy book about Dorothy and her dog, Toto, leaving Kansas. Judy Garland played Dorothy in the movie.

It cost a lot of money and was very hard to make movies in color at first, so most movies were still made in black and white for a long time after 1939.

But that's another story.

Movies are magic because they can bring our dreams to life – and in color!

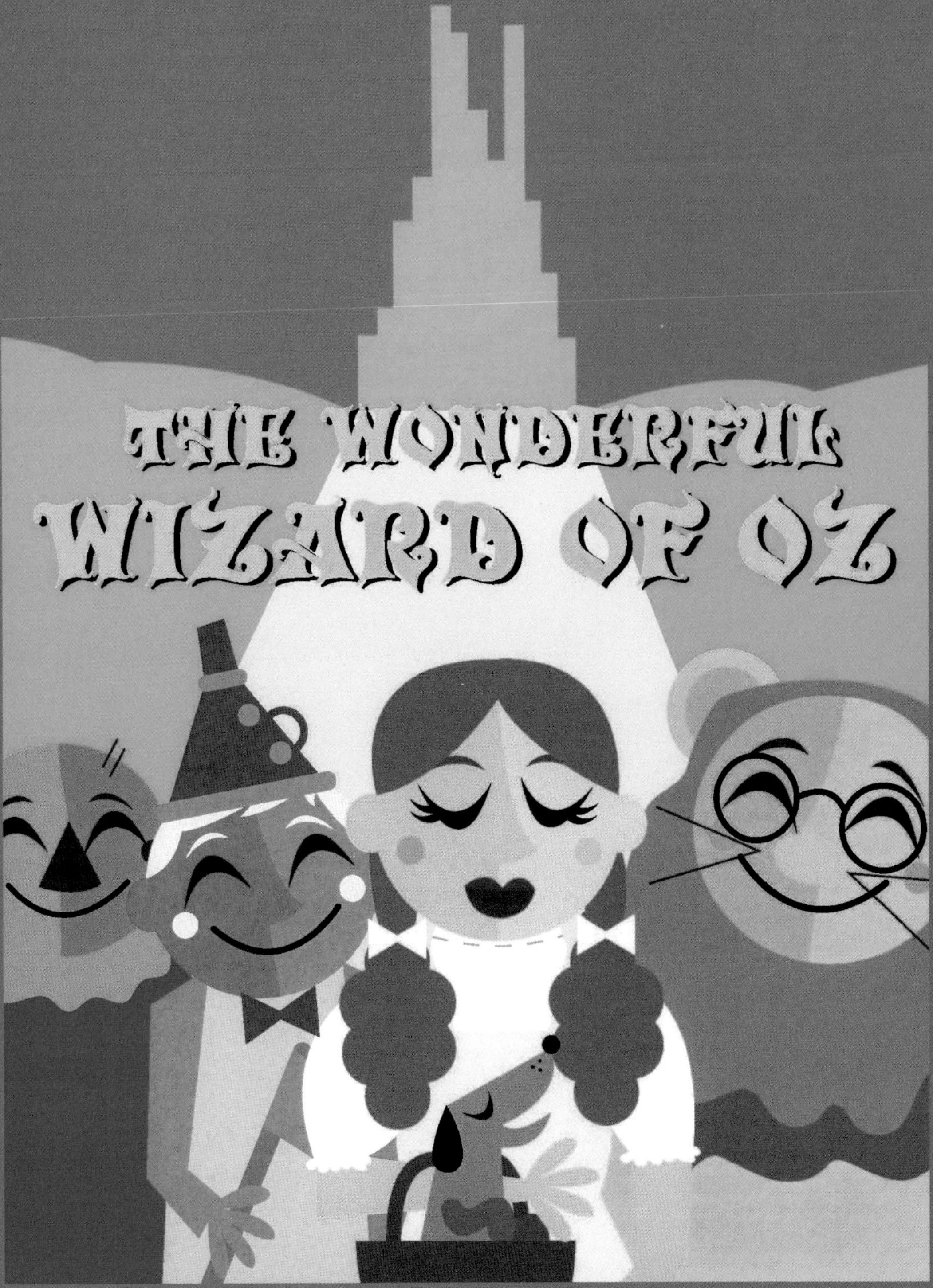
THE WONDERFUL
WIZARD OF OZ

NOTE FROM THE AUTHOR

Classic movies have a relevant place in our fast-moving, media-drenched world. These works of art connect us to the past, transport us to another time, and help us understand history and ourselves. This book is meant to grow with a child, and to help spur an interest in both kids and their parents to learn more about classic movie history. And, I hope, watch these movies together.

There's a linear connection that runs from the still and moving images captured more than 100 years ago to the YouTube videos, movies and video games that we watch on hand-held and electronic devices today.

Understanding this connection is crucial to developing media literacy, and to internalizing the history of storytelling through this magical, visual medium.

Thank you to the hundreds of people who supported the concept of this book, including but not limited to:

Andrew Alonso, Janice Beavers, Patrick Churchill, Sandro Corsaro, Lori Cunningham, Michelle Cunningham, Jennifer Dorian, Julie Ferris, Weston Gilmore, Garrett Hill, Phil Howell, Jennifer McHenry, Dr. Andrew Jefchak, Kristi Jeffrey, Lauren Jeffrey, Alison Kelly, Ben Mankiewicz, Heather Margolis, Eva Marie Saint, Steve & Vicki Siegrist, Vicki Stouffer, Vicki Whiting, Steve Woloszyk, and Kirsten Brundage Woodbury.

Movies - particularly classic movies - truly are magic.

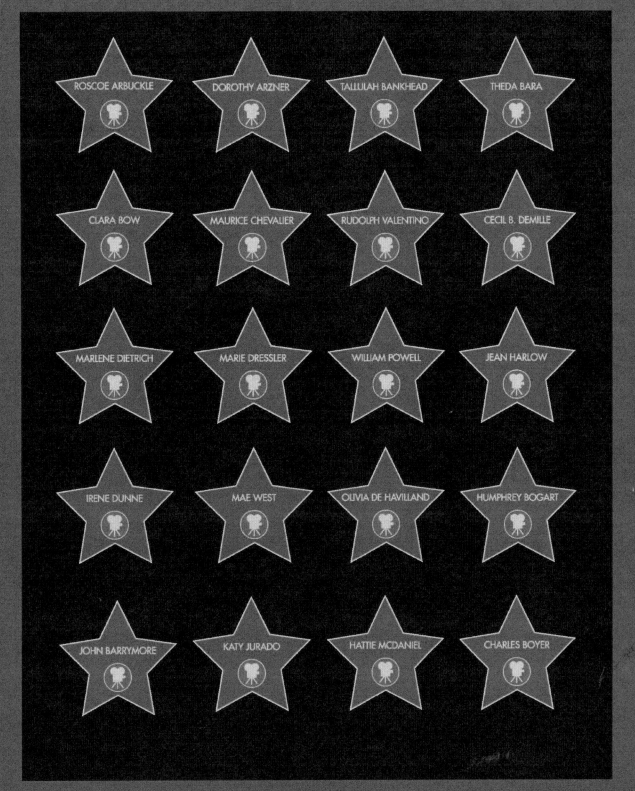

Made in the USA
Columbia, SC
20 September 2019